Mike Peyton's cartoons are a regular feature in yachting magazines all over the world. Five books of his cartoons have been published in this present series, *Come Sailing* (1975), *Come Sailing Again* (1976), *Hurricane Zoe and Other Sailing* (1977), *Finish with Engines* (1979) and *They Call it Sailing* (1981). There have been editions in several languages. Throughout the year he runs a 38 foot ketch, *Touchstone*, taking out charter parties, who provide him with many of his ideas, and operating from Maldon, Essex, where he owns a share of a boat yard. With his wife Kathleen, a best selling author, he lives at Fambridge on the north shore of the River Crouch.

The Pick of Peyton

Mike Peyton

NAUTICAL BOOKS
MACMILLAN LONDON

ISBN 0 333 33501 5

Published in Great Britain by
NAUTICAL BOOKS
an imprint of Macmillan London Ltd
4 Little Essex Street
London WC2R 3LF

Associated companies throughout the world

Filmset by Rowland Phototypesetting, Bury St Edmunds
Printed in Hong Kong

Contents

Publisher's note

This book contains those cartoons which Mike and myself would like reprinted and preserved from his five books all published by Nautical. These are now all out of print and were *COME SAILING, COME SAILING AGAIN, HURRICANE ZOE AND OTHER SAILING, FINISH WITH ENGINES and THEY CALL IT SAILING.*

The written material is by permission of the editors of the magazines where it originally appeared: *YACHTING AND BOATING WEEKLY, YACHTING MONTHLY* and *YACHTING WORLD.*

Peter Johnson

Foreword

by Carl Giles of the Daily Express

I was once 'enjoying' a wet and even more disastrous sail than usual. The great Uffa Fox was at the helm of a Flying Fifteen with myself, trying to be at my best in the presence of the Master, and making as big a cock-up with the sheets as it was possible to make. The last oaf aboard had not tied a knot in the jib sheet, and it took me half an hour getting it back from mid-air with a boat hook. By the time I had got things more or less straightened out we had arrived. "Drop 'em!" called Uffa. That went wrong as well.

Ashore, feeling as bleeding as my shins, and stammering excuses and apologies, I felt Uffa's hand on my shoulder as he said: "Gilsey, I've been sodding about in boats for over seventy years, and every time I go out I find something else that can go wrong."

Dear kind Uffa!
At least fifty Peyton calamities had happened on that one short sail.

I like drawing sailing cartoons but nearly always abandon the idea because I know I could not make it funnier than Peyton. If I do draw one about boats which is passably funny, I usually meet somebody who laughs then says: "Peyton did a beauty on that theme two or three years ago."

If there *are* any sailing riff-raff who have not yet met Peyton's beautifully drawn humour, his latest book gives them an opportunity now.

A little bit better than work

I would like to say right at the beginning that I *have* to write this. When an editor says 'Write fifteen hundred words on being a cartoonist' one writes – although it is all right for him, like drawing the bubbles above some character's head and saying, 'Put something witty in it'. It isn't as if cartooning is a cut-and-dried occupation. It's a full-time occupation in the true sense, but nebulous. The only definite thing I know about my next cartoon is that it is wanted in three days' time, but where it is and what it is doing at the moment I haven't the faintest idea. My last resort if the muse does not strike me is to go and sit in the bath and think. There have been times I have been in there so long that I have emerged as wrinkled as a dried prune and once or twice my wife has knocked on the door to check that she still has a husband. But up to now it has always done the trick.

In the ideal world ideas are handed to you on a plate. To give an example. I was delivering a boat one winter and the conditions were such that I was counting the minutes to the next watch appearing in the hatch. It was everything sailing shouldn't be. We were late on our tide, snow was driving in from the west, cold as I've known it, and the only sign of man was the flash of the lighthouse below Beachy Head. My relief took the tiller and clipped himself on. Surveying the cold miserable world about him he remarked, 'You know, Mike, sometimes sailing is only just a little bit better than work'. I drew it straight. These are the best ideas in all respects.

Some of the best ideas you see or hear would need a strip cartoon to explain them, or else they are too literal. There was a telling account of an ocean racer punching along on an especially dark and blowy night. You needed little imagination to picture the skipper and crew clambering between deck and cabin as they drove along. After losing two torches somewhere in the cockpit, the skipper asked, 'Can *anyone* put their hands on a torch?' It was a girl member of the crew who found it. 'Here it is!' She pushed it towards him, their hands met in the darkness and he found himself trying to switch on a cucumber.

Some ideas would definitely be better on film. I did manage to condense one such idea into a cartoon, but movement would have done it more justice. The yachtsman to whom this happened was chugging down the river under engine. He was alone on board and, to his horror – his first thought was of the supernatural – his mainsail started going up. He stood transfixed as it smoothly went up the mast. Then the engine stopped and all was made clear. The mainsail halyard had slid over the side and the end had wrapped itself round the shaft. Everything was back to normal: no engine and the mainsail fixed halfway up. . . .

Another incident that would be best shown on film was told to me by a water bailiff on the Norfolk Broads. You could say it was the classic situation: a strong current, too much wind, an inexperienced skipper and the yacht, or accident, looking for somewhere to happen. Fate chose a bend where a dozen or so yachts were moored up. Our skipper careered down the lot, crunching and cracking and wrenching, leaving doom and disaster in his wake. He finally brought up jammed into the bank where the bailiff found him. The bailiff got the name of the firm he had hired the yacht from and surveyed the mess – broken boom, torn sails, dangling stanchions and planks stove in. 'I'll call your hire firm and let them know the damage.' It was then that the unfortunate skipper's wife put her head through the hatch and put it all in perspective. 'And while you're about it tell them the fridge isn't working either.'

But normally, if that is the correct word, cartooning is simply a matter of seeing an everyday happening and just giving it a twist. I once watched a yachtsman coming ashore over a number of boats alongside each other. He was stepping over the guardrails and always, as a well-mannered sailor should, forward of the mast. On one small yacht the forward hatch was open and he idly glanced down. What he said I have no idea, but I drew it pretty well as near as I saw it, except that I had him lifting his hat and captioned it, 'I beg your pardon, Madam'. This is what I would call a typical idea, something that every sailing man or woman can relate to. An everyday event: you just add to it. I have seen hundreds of yachtsmen coming ashore over moored-up yachts but then one day I saw it differently and bingo! – an idea. Why it happens I cannot say.

Occasionally ideas come from entirely unrelated sources that have nothing to do with boats. One idea that falls into this category was literally dredged up from my past. During the last war when I was a keen young soldier (I gave the wrong age to get in) I was in a Recce battalion and one day with a companion I found myself in the path of two German tanks. We made ourselves as small as possible in what seemed a very small depression in the ground and circumstances were such that my companion asked, 'What comes after "Our Father who art in Heaven"?' Although I knew, I refused to tell him the answer, on a matter of principle, arguing that if he had to cut it as fine as this before he started to make his peace with his Maker he didn't deserve any assistance from anybody, let alone me. Perhaps I was being smug, but as this theological argument was going on the two tanks squeaked and rattled their way past us, one on either side. We hadn't been seen and the argument became irrelevant as we lived to fight another day. Heaven only knows what went on in my mind that caused it to recall that incident from so many years before and transpose the situation into the cockpit of a small boat, obviously in dire straits, with one of the two occupants saying to his companion, 'What comes after "Our Father who art in Heaven"?'

As you must now realize, cartooning as a way of making a living has its drawbacks (no pun intended). Unlike other occupations, whereas a farmer has land, a shopkeeper stock, bricklayers a pile of bricks, etc, cartoonists have nothing concrete, but just lots of intangible thoughts, feelings and emotions. A drawing of a skipper relaxing on a Baby Blake is no cartoon but if emotions are running high elsewhere on the boat, in the cockpit for instance, so that you caption it, 'Mummy, mummy, look out! Daddy!!' – you are there.

So what you need is an open mind, editors who bully you (in the nicest possible way, of course), a deadline to keep you at it, and best of all you just have to keep getting the seatime in, even if sometimes it is only just a little bit better than work.   M.P.

Yachtmasters all

'*As far as I'm concerned the Bretons can have Brittany.*'

'*According to my calculations, there's plenty of water.*'

'We should be seeing land in precisely three and a
quarter hours.'

'Dear Captain Sankey: I took your correspondence course in seamanship and navigation and passed with honours . . .'

'Just keep her jogging along while I have a recap.'

'Course I speak bleedin' English, where do you think
you are?'

'Decided what courtesy flag we want, Skip?'

'And after you've got the matches, just ask casually what lighthouse it is.'

'There's the East Knock.'

'And stop saying if I was at the navigation class I could ask Mr Hitchins.'

Making a meal of it

We had just finished lunch, my wife and I, when the phone rang. 'It's the yard here.' I live close to the yard. 'The engineer wants to know what is the trouble with your engine?'

'Hang on. I'll come down.'

I told my wife, who replied, 'Don't forget, Vic and Lena are coming at eight for a meal.'

'Don't be ridiculous', said I huffily. 'It's not two o'clock yet.'

'I'm not being ridiculous. I am simply reminding you that Vic and Lena are coming over at eight o'clock.'

I drove the couple of miles to the yard, in a manner of speaking, on my high horse. I rowed Dick the engineer down to the boat on the ebb tide. The sun was shining and I thought, 'What more pleasant way to spend a couple of hours mid-week than pottering on the boat?' On board Dick made his diagnosis.

'It looks as if that dog has jammed in the starter motor. We'll have it off.'

And so we started. We moved the batteries on to the cabin sole, and as I moved the second one I knocked the box of tools over. All the tools spilled out and one, and one tool only, went into the bilges, a small moveable.

Dick nodded morosely. 'That's it.'

I put the batteries on a bunk and pulled up the boards.

'We could do with a small tommy bar. Have you got one?'

I have and I keep it under the bunk. I moved the batteries again, and it wasn't the starter motor.

'It's inside. I can probably fix it from behind.'

Behind is also below the cockpit. Together we started on taking up the cockpit floor. Screw-heads broke off; the quarter-round broke. Dick finally disappeared down the hole. He was down a long time, and quiet, ominously quiet. He emerged.

'I still can't get at it. We'll have to move the engine forward.'

We disconnected holding-down bolts, fuel line, water, throttle, exhaust, drive. Floor boards up, batteries on forward bunk, oil and grease marks everywhere. We moved the engine forward, down the hole, up from the hole, not far enough. More levering, more straining, more oil, more grease, more curses, back down the hole, up from the hole, will not go any farther, sump in the way. We must lift. Look up at the open hatch, some four by four across.

'Unship the mainsail. I have some four by four.'

I went to get the four by four. It was forward under the bunk with batteries on. Restraining myself from manhandling them through the forehatch and dropping them over the side, I transferred them to the port bunk and all the rest of the gear that was with them, and got the four by four.

On to the next problem; make slings under engine, transfer main sheet, wrong lead, take off, reverse, replace choc-o-bloc. Wants raising, not enough height. More four by four. No four by four. Use bunk-boards. It takes longer to do than write. Still not high enough. I remembered the old service adage – when in doubt, brew up – so I lit the stove and put the kettle on. Sitting on the cross-members in the midst of chaos, our feet in the bilges, we ruminated, while the engine squatted there, dominating the saloon like some vast armoured creature halfway out of its black lair.

It was obvious that what we had to do was to get the boat alongside the stage and use the crane. We had no engine or sails, as the main sheet now had the engine on it. The work boat was moored up for the night and the yard men gone home. In the gathering gloom I got out a line to tow the boat from the dinghy. I rowed off and took the strain. Dick cast off and it started to rain. We had our little crises, natural to manoeuvring a 33 ft boat through crowded moorings with a good tide running – this was inevitable but we managed until we ran aground barely 20 feet from the landing and the crane. I made my line fast ashore and rowed back. We would just have to wait for water.

'I'm sorry,' Dick said, 'I'll just have to leave you to it. I'm taking the wife out.'

I rowed him ashore, returned on board and went below to shelter from the rain. Getting below was an operation in itself, squeezing under the lash-up of a hoist we had made over the engine. Once below, it was lethal, absolute chaos. The floor-boards were up and anything that you could put a foot on was covered in oil or grease. Gear and tools, warps and wood, were everywhere. It seemed as if everything that could be moved on the boat had been moved, and it was black as pitch. With no lights I pulled out the Tilley lamp. It was empty. I knew where the paraffin was – where it always was – forward under the port bunk, the one with the batteries on. By the time I had got the paraffin and lit the lamp there was enough water to warp the boat alongside the stage. I went through the drill in the darkness – bowline, stern-line, head warp, stern warp, springs . . . unshackle the main halyard for masthead line, fenders over the side and planks. All I had to do was turn out the Tilley lamp and go home. I jumped into the cockpit. In mid-air I remembered that it no longer had a floor.

If anyone else had been there they would have said, 'Gosh, you were lucky!' And I suppose I was but, straddling that cross-member, I didn't think so then. I climbed painfully back on to the bridgedeck and looked below through the tangled web of lines and timber. I could have wept at what I saw: it was everything a boat shouldn't be. I left the Tilley to burn itself out and drove home.

If ever a man needed a drink I did. The pub was closing as I arrived. I pressed on, incensed. They do say accidents are caused by bad temper and I can believe it. I screeched round the bend into the lane. Very little traffic uses it by day let alone at night – it was only the quick reactions of the driver of the white Mini which took off into the hedge that prevented the accident then. I roared on and stormed into the house.

'Some idiot in a white Mini nearly saw me off!'

'Yes', replied my wife. 'That would be Vic and Lena.'

Then my troubles really started.

D.I.Y.

'Between you and me, I don't think the boat show is our scene.'

'It's fired!!'

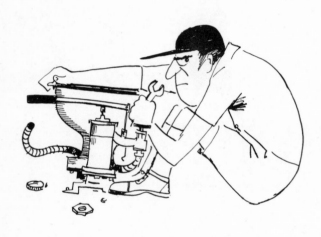

'And hurry up.'

'*I simply told her I wasn't kitted out to make a kitchen shelf and she went spare.*'

'*Have you any other interests?*'

Down with fitting out

Fitting out is all things to all men. I know men, and I have no doubt you do too, who fit out constantly from one laying up day to the next one, 12 months later. That is how they get their pleasure and good luck to them. They have got it made.

But this article is not for them. I'm not keen on fitting out. Boats, to my way of thinking, are for sailing in, not working on, and I have devoted a lot of thought on how to avoid fitting out.

The Victorians obviously had the answer: paid hands. I have often thought how pleasant it would have been to have sailed in those distant days if it wasn't for the nagging doubt that I would probably have been the paid hand.

Once you have started thinking about doing away with fitting out, or at least keeping it down to manageable proportions, a lot of obvious ideas spring to mind.

Stainless steel is one idea, and if you can afford it, it must pay off over the years in the way of stainless rigging, bottle screws, pushpits etc. Alloy spars are another time saver – admittedly varnished ones look more nautical but masts are for pulling sails up, not sanding down. Any gear you can do without, do without.

Everything that goes on a boat needs some time spent on it and these suggestions are just scratching the surface, but anyone who has had a boat long enough to fit it out can tell you more.

What you have to do is to look at the problem in a much wider sense. Ask yourself the question, 'Why do I fit out?' The answer is because you laid up. The problem is solved. Don't lay up and you won't have to fit out. It is as simple as that.

Commercial craft do not lay up. Fitting out, if you can call it that for them, is a constant process to keep the boat shipshape and seaworthy. Modern materials and marinas lend themselves to this method of keeping a yacht or power boat fitted out and ready for sea.

A present-day GRP cruiser tied up in a marina or a mudberth with alloy spars, stainless rigging, synthetic sails with a good sail cover and an engine and electrics that get a regular spray of some moisture repellant gives you the best of both worlds. You go when the going is good, work when south cones are hoisted.

British weather isn't geared up to set periods for fitting out and laying up. Statistically the traditional months for fitting out are among the windiest and wettest of the year. Winter months, on the other hand, can often offer you some good sailing days, even if they are a bit on the short side.

The long evenings when you are tucked away in some sheltered anchorage you can spend doing jobs below. Besides your tools you must also carry paint, varnish and brushes on board. You can get more painting done and a better job made of it in a couple of hours on a warm, windless day in June than in a month of wet weekends in the winter.

Good painting and varnishing weather is when you are shirtless and wearing shorts, preferably in some foreign harbour.

Another aid towards making fitting out merge into the general pattern of keeping the boat always ready for sea, rather than bringing it up to a peak condition like a horse being trained for some specific race, is to have some form of heater on board. You'd probably think twice about going to the boat if you knew the cabin was going to be as I once heard it described 'a cold, dark, damp box'. With some form of heating below you could be warmer and more comfortable than at home, which is susceptible to power cuts.

Spreading the load is another method of doing away with fitting out. You get volunteers down to do a weekend's work in return for a weekend's sailing. To look at it dispassionately as a time and motion exercise, if two people help you over one weekend then they and you are going to do more work in one weekend than you yourself will do in two. If three people help you the gain is all yours. So you work one weekend and sail the next with an easy conscience. If you give them a good sail they will probably sign on again.

The point to bear in mind, if you get people down to work for you, is to ensure that the work programme is mapped out beforehand and all the tools and materials are ready and at hand so that they can get on with the job. If they have to wander off to get some screws, buy timber or wash paint brushes then it's your fault, not theirs.

Another habit that is worthwhile cultivating in keeping fitting out to the minimum is to do jobs as they occur through the season as quickly as possible.

It is bad policy to say, 'I will leave it until I lay up'. Keeping a boat ready for sea is a constant process. The point to remember is that the boat is there to give you pleasure and if your pleasure comes from sailing it, you must concentrate all your effort and energy on keeping it seaworthy.

The cussedness of life is such that the more a boat is used the more work needs doing to it and, conversely, the less it is used, the less attention it needs but the more it seems to get.

There are three other suggestions I know of which can cut down fitting out. One definitely reduces the effort needed, but you won't do it: get a smaller boat. The second we can all hope for: a bigger bank balance so that we can give the yard carte blanche. The final one is what a friend of mine did for a number of seasons and I can vouch for its effectiveness but again I doubt if you will do it.

His method was simple and unique and he still got his sailing in. All he did was to sell his boat at the end of the season and buy new at the beginning of the next one. He was very honest about his advertising. You may have seen them, they invariably had the phrase in them 'in end-of-season order'. The only trouble was that when he came to buy he was a sucker for phrases such as 'yard maintained', 'stored under cover', 'yacht finish' etc.

The feminine touch

'Don't darling me!'

'Ready about!!'

'I've looked it up. Blue and white checks: No!'

'I see he has his bird down this weekend.'

'And if you tell me again it's the one sport we can do as a
family . . .'

'If we get back and they make a film of it I guess they'll
write another woman into it and make you black.'

'I beg your pardon, Madam.'

'And stop calling it a holiday!'

'I know you say you sail to get away from your wife,
but surely she can't be as bad as this?'

In the watches of the night

'Sure we'll contact Nader, but what are we going to do now?'

'Civilization all right, Bob, I can read the signs: Drugs, gas, eats, topless . . .'

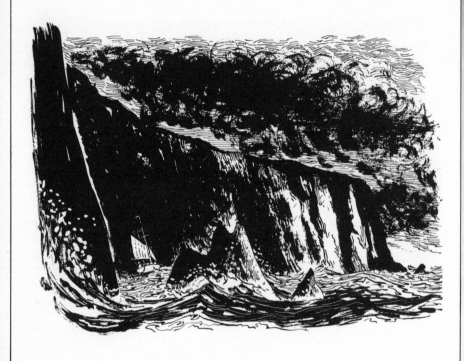

'The Pilot just says "A delightful anchorage in settled conditions".'

'Relax, Henry, that's the starboard hand beacon. I
know where we are to the inch.'

'What comes after "Our Father who art in Heaven"?'

'And I wish I was watching the midnight movie.'

'It's a conical; ease your sheets and run off.'

'On a night like this it's a lifesaver.'

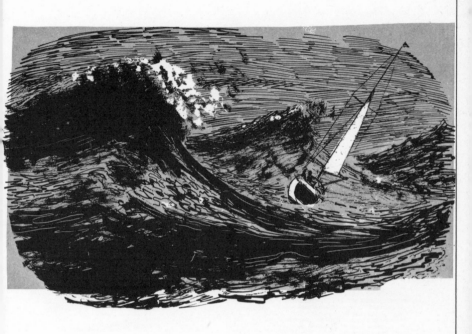

'There are times when I miss the old rat race.'

'But Pauline, I thought you liked sailing!'

'*Before you turn in, left is port is red. Correct?*'

Fog and fascination

I have always liked the story of the two shoe salesmen who were sent to some remote quarter of Africa. One of them immediately wired his head office, 'Returning at once. No one wears shoes out here.' The other salesman also wired his head office, 'Send all the shoes you can. No one wears shoes out here'. The same situation – it's just the way of looking at it that matters.

I am not saying that I look on sailing in fog with the same enthusiasm as the super salesman, nevertheless it does give one the opportunity of some fascinating navigation. Fog is not solely a winter phenomenon, so it can be enjoyed (if that is the right phrase) in the summer months. In the North Sea, May and June have the highest proportion of foggy days. The sea is still cool then and fog can occur when warm and damp air arrives over a cold surface. Fog is also associated with calm days, but this is not always the case. You can get windspeeds up to about 10 knots in fog. But as a general rule when there is fog the sea is calm, so one can concentrate on the navigation and not worry about sailing the boat.

Conditions were such when I had a trip in thick fog in February one year. It was a trip we had done often, nevertheless our capabilities were stretched. We were in Harwich and bound for Bradwell, 25 miles away. I had a charter party of six on board and fortunately they were keen, so it didn't take long to convince them how fortunate they were to have such a gift from the gods (all lies!).

The boat, *Lodestone*, is an Alan Hill designed 40ft centreboard ketch with a 31 hp Lister diesel engine. And, while we're on statistics, an official fog brings the visibility down to 1100yd (slight), 220yd (thick), and 55yd (dense). Moored alongside in

Harwich, we had points of reference and we knew we had dense fog to start with. The accepted norm of cruising – leave harbour and lay a course – went by the board. We had to get out of harbour first. In the main this was simply the application of common sense. We kept land-based noises on our starboard hand (traffic mainly) and used moored boats which were lying to the last of the ebb to direct us out. Because of the bends in the big ship channel, buoys are plentiful off the entrance to Harwich and I couldn't see us getting out without seeing one – in fact hitting one was my biggest worry – and we only wanted one.

We found it and circled it while a course was laid off. The log was streamed, time noted, and away we went. What we were after in this nebulous world we were travelling in were constants – anything definite to hang our position on. Already we had two: a definite point of departure, and a line on the chart – our course. After running a mile we had another one to add to these: our speed through the water. I had impressed everyone that the throttle control of the engine was not to be touched after leaving the buoy. We could also add the depth.

Running my boat as a charter boat I find it is often difficult to keep everyone occupied. One way I have is to heave a lead-line instead of using an echo-sounder. And so we settled into our routine. We had a lookout in the bows and a leadsman with one arm round the mizzen shrouds. My lead is marked off in knots, one for one fathom, two for two and so on, and – used by the mizzen – easily seen by the helmsman. Every 15 minutes there was switch over, a new lookout in the bows, the old lookout to the lead-line, the leadsman to the tiller and the helmsman went below.

On this run we crossed courses with history. Once Nelson, wanting to be in the Channel, had been held up in Harwich by a north-easterly which prevented his unhandy ships from getting round the Cork sands. One of his captains, in command of the *Medusa*, told him he could get him out over the Stone Banks on a southerly course, so they must have sounded their way over the same sands as we were negotiating as we made for the Medusa Buoy. We altered course before we had reached it and laid a course for the end of Walton pier.

When we had almost run our distance to the end of the pier I asked the lookout to start shouting. This may not be in books of coastal navigation but in all the years I have been sailing I have never seen a pier without a fisherman on it. A foggy day in February was no exception. The lookout's shout brought an answering hail.

'Is that Walton pier?'

'Yes!'

Feeling we should be polite:

'Any fish about?'

'A few cod!' and we were away. We altered course to run down the coast on the two-fathom line. It was here, casting the lead from the mizzen, that it paid off for the helmsman to be able to see the lead-line: over two fathoms he turned to the north and under two fathoms slightly south. We had about six miles of this to Clacton pier before I could see if my assumption about the fishermen of England held true.

It did. He was a more spirited one this time. In reply to the lookout's 'Hullo there!' came:

'Hullo yourself!' then continued, 'Who are you?'

'We're on a boat.'

'I know you're on a bloody boat. You'd be in a bloody bad way if you weren't.' The voice faded.

Here we left the line of soundings, which had been rather like having one foot on the pavement. (In *The Riddle of the Sands* Carruthers refers to the Itzendorf Flat as a handrail.) The nearest buoy that would serve was the Priory Spit, some three miles away, but to my way of thinking the North Eagle, four miles away, would be a better bet. There were logical reasons for this. The Priory Spit, the nearer buoy, was surrounded by soundings of much of a muchness, but the North Eagle had water of varying depths about it. In fact half a mile before it there was an increase in depth of over two fathoms. If we couldn't find that we deserved to be lost. If we did miss the North Eagle a mile beyond it on almost the same course we should be close to the North West Knoll. Also the tide would have less influence as it would be almost behind us, because of the slighter angle of the North Eagle to the coast. It gave us two good chances, especially as the fog was not so dense now.

We did not need the second chance. We picked up the North Eagle almost on the nose. By now the crew had a good appreciation of the job in hand. They were conscious of the vast moving carpet we were on, and the importance of the points of reference given by their soundings. On their watch off, they could look at the chart where the whole exercise was an abstract problem which made them appreciate the importance of the jobs they were doing – steering a straight course, taking regular soundings. Our next mark was the Bar Buoy, which we found easily by picking up the bar it marks with the lead.

Here off the mouth of the River Colne I was reminded of a fog story a friend of mine told me. In those days he was skipper of a motor barge. He was carrying his tide down the Colne bound for London; the Spitway was farther east in those days and had less water, and he was pressing on as well as the dense fog would allow, being short of time. And it *was* dense, because as he was passing the area where shipping for Colchester brings up to wait for the tide to take them up, his crew, who was standing outside the wheelhouse, was hit on the top of his head by a lighted cigarette stub. The point is he never saw where it came from, and you can't flick a cigarette end very far.

A run of a mile with the tide directly behind us and consequently no allowance to make – always a bit of a guess, brought us to the Bench Head, and then the next five miles were on soundings again. By now darkness had fallen and, together with the fog, visibility was virtually nil. Even 15 minutes on lookout was miserable enough, and by the time the lookout had seen anything we would have hit it anyway. But it was worthwhile continuing with the precaution, as a lookout hears things sooner than anyone else, being farthest from the engine. What I was worried about now was hitting the jetty that lies a little way offshore at Bradwell, so before we had run our distance I decided to drudge. We handed the log, the anchor went over the bows and as I stopped the engine we got an unexpected bonus. In the unaccustomed silence aboard we could hear the faint hum of the turbines at Bradwell power station. We took a bearing.

Drudging is a slow business, so I unshackled the anchor and drudged with chain alone. I reckoned it slowed us sufficiently, but not as much as the anchor would have done. It hadn't got the built-in safety factor that is there with the anchor shackled on, so we put the dinghy on a long line and let it drift ahead of us, a sort of early warning system. I thought we would hear if it hit anything and we would have time to press the starter button. Slowly the bearing on the hum of the turbines altered. When it bore 150° we anchored, had a meal and turned in. We awoke to a hazy dawn, fifty yards off the entrance beacon into Bradwell and inshore of the jetty.

I would be the first to admit that feeling your way through the fog lacks the attraction of crashing along in a good breeze, but sailing has uncountable fascinating facets and I think a thick fog can provide some of them.

Below decks

'*Keep her on this tack, Peter, until I serve the soup.*'

'What's set you off?'

'That's funny, my wife complained about the toilet
arrangements too.'

'Put the purée into an earthenware casserole, with the
juice of the lemon and the hearts of three cooked
artichokes, sauté the liver . . .'

'Mummy! Look out!! Daddy!!!'

'Get that spinnaker up.'

'I know we didn't do it like this at nav classes . . .'

'You're on, boy.'

PEYTON

'Not on the chart!'

'Escapism from what?'

'I'll give you three guesses which one we want.'

'Do you ever wonder why we do it, Douglas?'

Cordon eau

'Watch it, the bottom of the dinghy is wet so hold it undern . . .'

'There's times I know I'm a cruising man at heart.'

*'Perhaps oilskins could be better designed but I'm glad
I've got mine on now.'*

'And to think it all started with a trial subscription to a
sailboat magazine.'

"Hold your course, John, we don't want to confuse him now."

"*Thinking of getting rid of the old Silhouette, then?*"

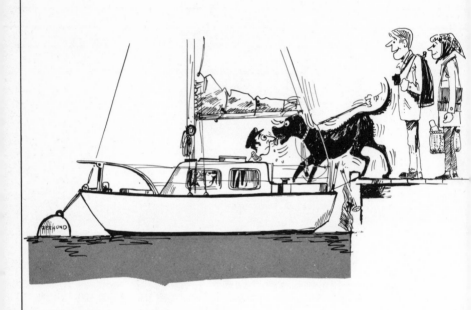

'We brought Bounder along, we knew you
wouldn't mind.'

'She's a better weight carrier than I thought!'

'You can't beat it, Tony, a good sail, a quiet drink, then
a row back in the moonlight to a snug little cabin.'

'If it is any consolation, Humber, Thames, Dover,
Wight are having 2 to 3 southerlies.'

'*Van de Velde*, Shipping in a gale off Ostend.'

'Bloody foreigners.'

'But I've got to go, I only came out to take the dog for a walk.'

'Don't get excited, darling, everything is under control.'

Those who sail
and those others...

Writing an article about the character of English yachtsmen for a foreign yachting magazine made me wonder, 'Are they any different from foreign yachtsmen, and if so, why?' I have come to the conclusion that they are and there is a reason. I think it can best be explained by a story told of Ulysses who, having returned to his native land after years of wandering, asked one of his veteran oarsmen what he was going to do now. The old sailor replied that he was going to put his oar over his shoulder and keep walking inland until someone asked him what it was he was carrying over his shoulder. 'There', said the veteran, 'I will settle down.' In England he would only have to walk about 100 miles and if he hadn't been asked by then he never would be because he would be getting closer to the sea on the other side.

The one thing England has plenty of is salt water and you cannot get more than 100 miles from it. Even the English language is linked to the sea. To give only one example: if a man is short of money in England it is said he is 'hard up', from a sailing boat being 'hard up on the wind', or it is said he is 'on his beam ends', again a nautical expression for a boat in dire distress, or again he is said to be 'on the rocks' which is self explanatory. Unlike more fortunate nationalities in better-designed countries who have mountains in which they can climb or ski, lakes to fish and forests to wander in, the Englishman either plays ball games or sails – there's nothing else.

The other great difference is that the English yachtsman is ruled by the tides. As I have said England is badly designed. Unlike the countries by the Baltic or the Mediterranean, where the yachtsmen sail at civilised hours, Britain is affected by tides. They sweep around and meet near Dover, every day at a different time, height and strength. If an English yachtsman has a boat that will sail at four knots and the tide that day is running at 1½ knots, you will see he will either travel at 2½ knots or 5½ knots depending on when he leaves his mooring. So he leaves when the tide serves. This invariably seems to be about 0200 and, as it rains a lot in England and you get lots of fog, you can appreciate why an English poet wrote that the English 'take their pleasures sadly as St. Lawrence took the grid'.

I have a friend who put his house up for sale. One evening there was a knock at the door and he answered it to find a man who said he was interested in buying the house. 'Well come inside and look around', said my friend.

'That won't be necessary', said the visitor. 'All I want to do is measure the space beside your house.' Taking a tape measure out of his pocket, he measured the area. He explained that he owned a boat and wanted a house with enough space alongside it to store his boat during the winter.

He finished his measuring, found there was enough space for his boat and said 'I will buy the house'.

'But don't you want to see inside?' asked my friend.

'Oh no, I am sure it will be all right, but my wife will be interested and I'm sure she will be along later.' This incident shows a thoughtful side to the character of the English yachtsman – that even when he was involved in the serious business of arranging winter storage of his yacht he still had time to think about the interests of his wife.

I know another yachtsman who rowed back to his boat one evening with his wife, having spent a few pleasant hours in the riverside pub. Just before he turned in for the night he was standing by the shrouds attending to the call of nature when he saw a yachting hat drifting by on the tide. 'Quick!' he called to his wife because he was engaged and could not do anything himself.

'Get the boat hook and catch this yachting cap!' Before his wife could do anything a voice from the darkness said, 'Never mind the bloody hat, catch me!' So they let the hat go and caught its owner, who was also being swept down on the tide, and dragged him up on board. This I think shows a helpful side to the yachtsman's character. They also gave the rescued man a drink to warm him up which shows friendliness and common sense, and when they rowed the owner of the hat back to his own boat he invited them on board and gave them a drink which shows gratitude and also that the English yachtsman likes a drink.

In fact if it hadn't been for drink this story would not have been told, because if it hadn't been for drink the man who told me the story would not have been standing by the shrouds at that critical moment. It may even be that if it hadn't been for drink the owner of the cap would not have fallen into the water.

Another yachtsman I heard of, a skipper, was in a race across the North Sea. The weather was foul with heavy rain and the wind fair but strong. They had a fast but uncomfortable sail. The finishing line was just off a harbour entrance and they crossed it as darkness fell. Immediately they had crossed the line, the skipper gave the order to harden in the sheets and, bringing the boat about, he started on the long beat back to England and the thunderstruck crew saw the welcoming lights of the harbour disappear in the murk.

Later the skipper gave his reasons for doing this. It was simply that they had had such a miserable trip across that if he let his crew put a foot onshore he wouldn't have got them back on board again. So he didn't give them the chance. Once in the old days when I was a crew member I would have said this showed a sadistic side to the skipper's character, but now that I am a skipper I am certain it shows that skippers know their crews.

Sailing plus!
I have a friend who owns an old gaff cutter. He is a very enthusiastic sailor and he got a great deal of pleasure out of it. Then he met a girl and got married. Shortly afterwards we met and he told me he had discovered one of the greatest joys that life had to offer. Naturally I smiled but I was also curious and asked for more details. He told me it was to have his old boat sailing itself offshore through the summer seas. I replied I thought this was a tremendous source of pleasure but not exactly new, but my friend had not finished and then there came the discovery that lifted the marvellous to the sublime.

It was to make love to his wife in the rubber dinghy which he carries lashed down on the cabin top. 'It's fantastic! Sailing plus!' This I think shows that the English yachtsman is very keen on sailing and also that he is very unselfish and willing to share the pleasures of sailing with others. (Incidentally, if you have a boat that sails itself, a rubber dinghy and a wife, it is best if the rubber dinghy isn't pumped up too hard, especially the bit you sit on.)

I have another friend who put his boat up for sale. He received a number of letters of enquiry about the boat, one of which came from a prison. The prisoner wrote that he had seen the advertisement and was certain that the boat for sale was just what he wanted. Unfortunately circumstances being what they were, he would not be able to look at the boat for himself. However, he would take my friend's word for it that everything he said about the boat was true. This I think shows the trusting nature of English yachtsmen. He went on to say that he would be able to pay in cash, but pound notes; the only drawback was that even with remission for good conduct it would be almost two years before he could get out to lay his hands on the money. It was unfortunate that my friend could not wait this long – some English yachtsmen also have an impatient side to their character.

Another story which will give some insight into the character of the AEY (Average English Yachtsman) I pieced together from what was told me by an AEY I know called John and his girlfriend, Pauline. They were sailing back to England from Calais in their 26ft plywood yacht. As I have mentioned earlier you sail when the tide serves and in this instance the tide served at 2300. Normally the crossing would take anything from four to five hours. The wind was strong, it was raining and, as always in the Channel, there was a lot of shipping about (300 ships a day pass through the Dover Straits). Pauline felt sick if she went below, so she was at the helm. John did the navigation, made cups of coffee and, as it was pointless him being outside in the cockpit getting wet and being uncomfortable, he laid down on a bunk. Sometime during the crossing when there was a little more shipping about than usual, the injustice of this got on top of Pauline and she lost her temper. John, dozing below, heard the shouting and thought she was in trouble. He pushed open the hatch and received the full blast of her fury. All he could say in reply was 'But Pauline, I thought you liked sailing!' This set her off again, 'You think I like sailing, sitting here soaked through in a gale of wind, scared stiff, in a stupid little boat that will be run down or turn over . . .' And so she went on.

Eventually they made harbour as usual and as usual all was laughed over so I got to hear their story and, as I draw cartoons on sailing subjects, I drew this incident. Simply a little boat in a rough sea at night and the caption, 'But, Pauline, I thought you liked sailing?' The upshot of this was that I received letters from other AEYs who had seen the cartoon and who said I must have got the idea from them because their wife or girlfriend was called Pauline. Now Pauline is not a very common name so I realized that if I had made the name Joan, I would have received a lot more letters. Which brings me to the conclusion that there is a flaw in the character of the AEY: he does not really understand the working of the feminine mind.

Weekend visits

There is no doubt that, once bitten by the sailing bug, the Englishman takes it very seriously and I know an AEY who bought a house solely because it was close to his boat. He lived just under a mile from his moorings. I met him one night and in the conversation it came out that he was moving from the area.

'The trouble is,' he said, 'living so close prevents me spending much time on the boat.' I professed that I could not see the reason behind this, so he explained.

'When you are so close to your boat you have no excuse for sleeping on board. After all, I could walk home in a few minutes.' As you can appreciate the AEY has a very logical mind.

Somewhat in a similar vein I met the wife of an AEY and naturally asked after her husband. She told me he had gone to visit their eldest son Andrew who was away at a boarding school. 'At least, that is what he says.' Being curious I asked why she had said that. 'Well, he has laid up his boat for the winter in a harbour about four miles from the school, and although he visits Andrew almost every weekend in the winter he hardly ever goes down in the summer.' As you can see from this incident the AEY is very interested in the education of his children, especially in the winter.

Finally I would like to tell you about a friend of mine who sails, an AEY who is also a surgeon. We were going out for an evening but first he had to call on three patients on whom he had to operate the following day. They were all in private nursing homes and he did not expect it would take long to visit them. We screeched to a halt at the first nursing home and he grabbed his stethoscope and dashed in. A couple of minutes later he was back and, as we rushed off to the next patient, he told me the one he had just seen was an oil sheik. The procedure was repeated, in and out within minutes; the patient that time a minister of some country. At the third call I never even switched off the engine but this time the minutes ticked by and it was quite a considerable time before he emerged.

I was curious. If he couldn't see anything of interest in an oil sheik and a foreign minister, what had kept him? I should have guessed.

'Very interesting case', he said as he got back in the car. 'He was reading a yachting magazine when I went in. He keeps a ten tonner at Burnham.' I rang up this friend once at the hospital and I was put through to the department where he worked. I was told he was in the operating threatre and unobtainable – 'Unless,' the voice at the other end of the line said, 'you are a sailing friend.' I visualized the surgeon picking up the phone with his gory rubber gloved hand and said, 'I will ring back', and put down the receiver. What I think these incidents show is that the AEY divides the world into two distinct halves, those who sail and those who don't. This I think is one of the greatest characteristics of the AEY. Any foreign yachtsman visiting England will realize this is true, because if he is on a boat he will be accepted by the AEY as an AFY. In fact when I think of it, I have met a few AFYs in my travels and I have always got on well with them. So I think it is probably true that there is no such thing as an Average English Yachtsman, or an Average Foreign Yachtsman, only average yachtsmen who speak different languages but think alike ... about boats!

Close encounters

'There's times, Bert, when life has little more to offer.'

'The last time I pulled this one he gybed all standing and broke his boom.'

'Hello Frank! I was just sailing over to say hello.'

'No, mate, there's no law against you lying there, only gravity.'

'*Starboard!!!*'

'We'll just stop a minute and work out exactly what's
happening below.'

'That's their gun. Lengthen the dinghy painter, sheet
in and we'll catch the lot on port.'

'I know anyone can put a boat aground, but only you
could put it aground here!'

'Look, there's that lovely couple we met in Cherbourg.'

'Watah! Watah!'

'I know I thought it was a good idea then, but I'm sober now.'

Safe in harbour

*'And from the looks of it, they'll have damn all to
declare, if we do get on board.'*

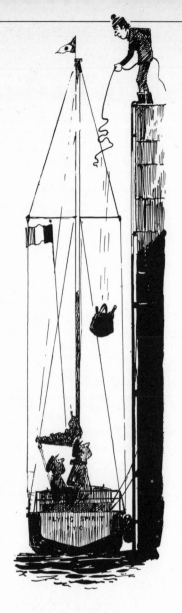

'Duty free coming dow . . .'

'Throw him a line!'

'She must be on the ground, she's leaning a little.'

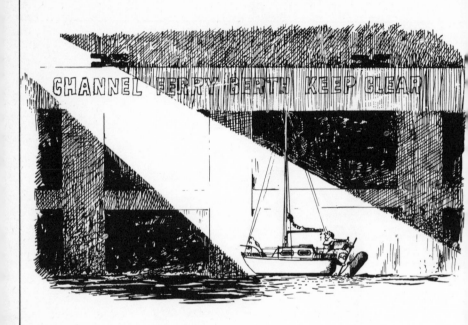

'It could be a rough trip.'

'Wants potty does he? He's not the only one.'

A new angle on cooking

Cooking on a boat has one ingredient which is never mentioned in any cookbook, and yet it is the deciding factor that determines any meal on board. It is the angle of heel. Moored up in a marina, you can devil, marinate or baste with the best. At the other extreme you have prayer and fasting; somewhere midway you have yacht cooking.

One thing which is surprising is the number of boats that have no decent provisions for making a meal under way, or catering for the angle of heel. In this respect I remember talking to a delivery skipper who spent most of his summer delivering boats from Dover to the Solent. Their owners, after running up the French coast from Cherbourg to Calais had crossed back to Dover and run out of time or into bad weather. He had done the trip down Channel innumerable times and his overall impression was that there was no provision to make even a cup of tea on the majority of boats.

Ideally meals cooked offshore should be appetising, filling, easy to prepare and leave no washing-up. Starting with breakfast, there is no doubt bacon and eggs is what comes to mind, yet it is not the simplest of meals to prepare. But it can be simplified. You start at home by cutting the rind off the bacon, a job of a few minutes there, but it seldom gets done on board. When the bacon is nearly cooked I break the eggs over it so that it becomes as one – my regulars call the end result bacon and egg nosh.

Two other simple breakfasts are kippers or sausages, which you can buy in plastic bags, merely dropping them in boiling water until they are heated through. (You can also get rice in plastic bags to cook like this.) Boiled eggs are simple and if you buy them in papier mâché egg containers you can use these as egg cups and save on washing-up. Cornflakes do not stay the distance on a boat, but there is one cereal, based on the Swiss muesli, called Alpen, which is a mixture of cereals, nuts and dried fruit – very concentrated and needs only the addition of milk – and is definitely worth a try. If you are conventional enough to finish with marmalade, the chunky type has a better resistance to heel.

Lunch on my boat is generally cold fare – cheese, tinned meat or salmon, or pork pies. A way of using a tin of salmon is to make up some powdered potato (boil the water and add the contents of the packet), then drop in the tinned salmon and mix. Bully beef also lends itself to this treatment. Simple to make, filling and it stays on the plate at a fair angle of heel.

Evening meals are invariably stews out of tins and I work on the ratio of one tin per head. Sometimes the combination has been out of this world but, by the time we have realized that we have hit on a cordon bleu combination, the recipe – six empty tins – has been full fathom five and we never seem to remember it again.

In a meal of all tinned food it pays to add something to give that little extra flavour, for tinned foods have an overall taste. If you are sailing in French waters, of course, a drop of *vin rouge* in the stew does the job marvellously. Curry powder can also do it, or fresh onion. If conditions allow it, meals don't necessarily have to be all that basic – you can help circumstances along too. To give an example, we were bound up Channel for Burnham and decided that Calais would be a worthwhile call for some duty-free. With an offshore wind we closed the coast and took advantage of the sheltered waters of Rye Bay to cook and eat a relatively elaborate curry in comfort. Washed up and stowed, we were ready for anything when we cleared Dungeness and when the fog came down and the wind came up it was just taken in our stride.

It is often well worthwhile advancing a mealtime or waiting a little (not too much) to allow you to take advantage of an alteration in course or the shelter of a headland. I remember one time we were bound for Le Havre – we were hard on the wind until we rounded Cap Gris Nez and the meal which would have been an effort to do to the east of Gris Nez was child's play on the south of it, and it was prepared and eaten in comfort.

The other way of getting a meal inside you when offshore is to heave-to – that is, if you have got a boat that will heave to, as nowadays this does not seem to be considered a virtue in a boat.

An odd thing about sailing, unlike walking, where people will stop and sit down for lunch and admire the scenery, is that yachtsmen always seem to be in a hurry. They leave one harbour and literally scurry to the next. If the wind eases or their speed drops below x number of knots, on goes the engine. They only seem to relax when they are swinging on a buoy or moored up fore and aft. Yet heaving to is probably the best way to have a meal at sea – one minute all bash and splash, and the next she is riding the seas like an empty detergent bottle. In a more distant and romantic age the simile was 'riding to the seas like a gull with her head under her wing'.

One of my strongest sailing memories is of the first time I was on a boat that hove to. I can still remember the owner of that little old gaff cutter saying, 'I think we'll stop for a cup of tea'. I also remember looking queasily at the tossing, turbulent world about us and thinking, 'If only we could!' And then we did, and came the revelation that in sailing you can in a manner of speaking stop the world if you want to get off. But very few yachtsmen take advantage of it nowadays.

I remember reading an article in an old yachting magazine on siting the galley. It started from the logical premise that, if possible, you always heave to on the starboard tack, so the galley should be to port. The point being that you are looking down on the stove and in case of anything happening it will fall away from you.

Oddly enough, one traditional meal for yachtsmen is far from being easy to prepare or wash up. This is mackerel or, in fact, any fresh fish that you cook on board. The only fish I have found simple to prepare on a boat was a salmon we had thrown on the deck from a Scottish fishing boat off the Northumbrian coast. We simply boiled it and had it cold with brown bread and beer. It was marvellous.

I have crewed on offshore racers where the catering was just a very large flask of coffee, and rolls. You simply helped yourself when you felt like it. If I am going on a boat with this system I like to take my own sandwiches, and they are always bacon ones – the reason being that I have them made while the bacon is still warm, so that the butter on the bread melts and then sets again, effectively joining together what a considerable amount of sculling around in the cockpit cannot tear asunder. For this type of commissariat, fruit, chocolate, nuts and raisins or cheese are ideal. But I think the cruising man can do better. The difference as I see it between the cruising man and the racing man is that the former is basically interested in the travelling, the latter in arriving. This is what affects their different attitudes to cooking on board.

The item that keeps the stove the warmest is drinks, and on this subject I would say get the biggest mugs you can. What will hold more will hold less, and the larger they are, the greater the angle of heel they will stand. It is the obvious thing to buy the mugs and design your own stowage round them, and when you are doing this it is worth trying to arrange the stowage so that the mugs themselves can be filled while stowed. Failing this, the best thing is to stand them on the gimballed stove so that they can be filled without spilling too much.

Having the mugs in different colours has one spin-off: if each person on board keeps the same coloured mug for the trip it is far easier for the cook of the moment to remember what goes in what. Red: one sugar and black; blue, two sugars and white, and so on. Keeping the containers that hold the makings of a cup of tea or coffee convenient to the stove is a sensible arrangement. Also it is worth bearing in mind that there are other drinks. I recollect the pleasant surprise of a helmsman one cold night when I handed him a cup of Oxo instead of the expected tea. Cocoa is another drink that goes down well.

There is one rule that I try to stick to on my boat, and that is that the cook does not wash up. This often falls down in bumpy weather as it often works out that the only one who can go below to cook is the only one who can stay below to wash up. It is worth trying for, however. Another point to bear in mind is that if you are not hungry, it does not follow that the other people on board are not hungry either. They might be just too polite to say so and you, as skipper, have a vested interest in keeping your crew well fed and ready for anything.

Napoleon's dictum that 'an army travels on its stomach' could easily be applied to yachtsmen.

Meanwhile back at the yard

'Now just keep it port side to, until I collect the deposit.'

'*Looks as if it will clear up for Monday.*'

'You might call it mutiny, we call it common sense.'

'Pity about the weather, Skip, when we were all geared
up to do a good weekend's work.'

'You wouldn't drive 40 odd miles in this weather just to
pat my bottom.'

'It's amazing to think she's only 22 ft overall.'

'Naughty Doggie.'

'Up again, Joe.'

Hard racing croppers

'I can hear them in the bar now "To Absent Friends!"
Haw . . . Haw . . . Haw.'

'Can you manage that gear all right, John?'

'Give 'em a bloody bearing and get this boat moving!'

'A smart bit of spinnaker work, boys. I reckon the race
is in the bag.'

'The results will still be there next weekend, and just as
soon.'

'And let me tell you, when he can tie a bowline and tell
port from starboard, we're out of a job.'

'Tread water, Jim, he was the one we beat in the protest
last weekend.'

"All the others left us to port!"

"I sometimes think that as a sport it's over-rated."

'We cannot stop, we're racing, but if you sail 270° for 32 miles you should be OK.'

'I admit it's unusual but he's flying no distress signals
and what's more to the point we're leading our class.'

'Permission to come on board, Skip.'

'. . . It's still pretty slack.'

"Relax son, these racing boys know what they're doing."

'All Class III boats – who's going to tell him?'

'Never mind what it reminds you of. Sort the bloody
thing out.'

'Hughie, Hughie, where the hell are you? The spinnaker
has twisted.'

'The only time this season we've been in front and you
don't know the bleedin' course!'

For times like this

There are times while you are sailing when life at that particular moment seems to move up on to a plane you hardly knew existed. You know when you are up there, you know when it is gone. I recollect four of us sharing such a time – unforgettable moments, in the true sense of the word. We still remember it years later.

We were on a gaff cutter bound for Ostende. It was Easter, the first sail of the season, and we had a 'topsail breeze' on the quarter and everything that that means to a beamy old gaffer. There was a moon out that you could read the chart by and we rolled along down its path. No one stood watches, no one turned in. We all knew we were living on the top line; no one was going to waste it. We did nothing spectacular – talked, smoked, made coffee. All of us at one time or another went and stood in the bows and looked back. I've done it often but that night was different. For some reason there was a heightened awareness of it all. The glow of the nav lamps, the odd spark from the bogey stove swirling away into the night, the murmur of voices from the cockpit, a laugh and all those indeterminable noises as a boat gets about its business.

Look aloft and there was a fantastic moving pattern of silvery (hackneyed but true) light and dark shadows changing and counter-changing as the boat dipped and swayed. Was that ethereal stuff up there really eight ounce cotton tanned and with more patches on it than I cared to think? Then came the dawn. The wind headed us, no one had had any sleep and the trip back was murder. We were hove-to off the West Hinder for hours and a boat that left at the same time, *Ally Sloper*, lost a man, washed out of the cockpit.

I have a friend, not a sailing man at the time, who still remembers vividly a spell at the wheel of an old schooner in heavy weather when life showed him what it could offer. The schooner was on charter to a group of his friends, skin divers. He was in his bunk half asleep one night as the old schooner, well reefed, crashed along just off the wind, and he imagined that he heard someone shouting. Someone in trouble? He went on deck. The skipper's girl friend, alone on deck, was at the wheel and she was shouting into the stormy night fit to burst her lungs. She saw him. 'Here try it, it's marvellous', and he took the wheel and it was marvellous – one minute dozing in a bunk, the next braced at the wheel, crashing along in a heaving, rolling world of wind and water and black as pitch. 'But you must shout.' 'Why?' 'Well, it fits in. Try it.' What does one say (shout) on occasions like this? A phrase came to mind – it had always seemed a bit forced when he had heard it previously but this seemed the time and the place. He filled his lungs and rolling the words around his tongue, bellowed into the turbulent night: 'Cry Havoc! Unleash the hounds of war!' He paused, she was right, it was marvellous, absolutely bloody marvellous. He filled his lungs again. 'Cry Havoc . . .' and as the old schooner crashed along they shouted themselves hoarse through the night. He told me he felt a bit embarrassed when he saw the girl the day after, but he has never forgotten and never will.

These incidents were brought to mind because recently life moved up a notch for me again. I was slicing tomatoes at the time and quite suddenly and certainly I knew I was away. Like a dinghy getting up on a plane, like going on 'a trip', I suppose. I was alone, bound for Toulon, and I had just passed two rocks with the apt name Les Deux Frères. They had been in shadow as I approached and had looked black and ominous and I remember thinking they could be Big Brothers too in the wrong conditions. But with them astern and now looking warm and friendly with the sun on them, I decided it was time for lunch. I lashed the tiller and went below. I have got into the habit now of noting where the sunshine is coming from immediately I go below. There was a patch conveniently sliding up and down on the chart table from the port above it, and I knew that as long as that patch stayed there *Lodestone* was behaving herself. I started slicing tomatoes and I knew I was, as a poet once put it ' . . . fifty thousand miles away from all the wheels that run, as one with wind and waterfall and swinging with the sun'. I wasn't doing anything special, just slicing tomatoes alone in the cool cabin of a boat that was moving smoothly and easily through blue waters, but for some reason there was this heightened awareness of everything about me.

From the cockpit I could hear the squeaking of the tiller line as it let me know it was doing all the work. The patch of sunshine was still backing and filling on the chart table. I seasoned my tomatoes, added a few olives, broke some bread off a long French loaf, and got an orange. I crossed the cabin to get myself a glass of *vin ordinaire* out of the locker and the scrap of carpet I have on half the cabin floor felt positively luxurious to my bare feet. I carried my meal up into the sunshine and stood in the hatch with my lunch alongside on the doghouse top. Life really had not a lot more to offer, a good boat going well, sea, sun, wine. In the distance was a headland, blue and hazy in the heat. I glanced down at the chart on the cockpit seat – barely four miles away. I wished it were forty-four.

I finished lunch and took the helm. This was what sailing was all about. How long it lasted I have no idea, but not long, for the headland was close when the wind fell light. I debated, then decided to change headsail. I stirred myself, stubbed my toe on the anchor and somehow life had slipped down a notch or two. It was still good, the sun still shone, the sea was still blue, but we were no longer in the heights. The drawback with a time like this is that you cannot save any of it. So much is wasted in its liberality: there is no way of stowing any away, preserving any, putting it in a fridge for periods 'laid up and out of commission'. It is probably for times like this we sail, but we get so few of them and there is no denying we earn them.

Home is the sailor

'He's out, working on his boat.'

'Westerly 36. Nicholson 30.'

'If he says he's had a Nicholson 32 in his stocking again,
I'll do him.'

'I tell you, he's from accounts.'

'Better take your "Quells", dear, schools out.'

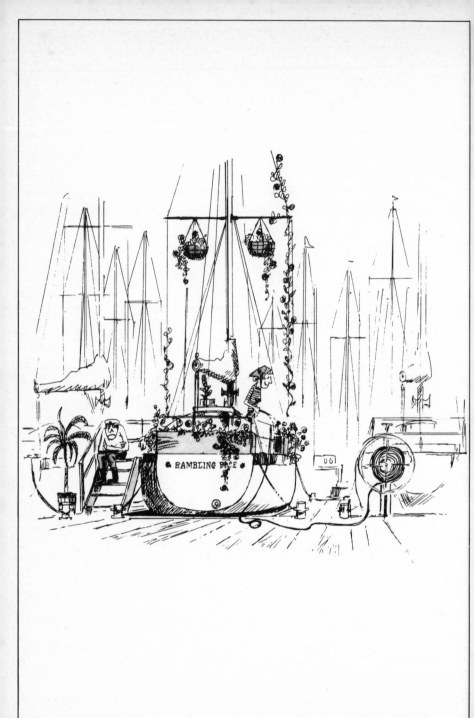

'I feel sick, dear – sea sick.'

'I say, old boy, if you're off the little cutter that picked
up the end mooring, you can't leave her there.'

'Have you no soul? Spring tides, high water, blowing
a gale, the boat in a mud berth, and all you think
about is . . .'

'I'm just warning you, don't slip out the back with any
of your pals for a look at the boat.'

'I don't know why you go to the Boat Show. You always come back miserable as sin.'

'Hello darling. I was just wondering if you felt like a run
down to the coast.'

'Are you coming in for your Christmas dinner, or shall I
leave it in the oven?'